HIGH FLIGHT

—— A STORY OF WORLD WAR II ——

LINDA GRANFIELD

Illustrated by Michael Martchenko

Tundra Books

For Jean Marmoreo, with gratitude – LG

For Patricia – MM

*And, with our deepest respect and appreciation, for all the airmen
in the skies and on the ground who dedicated their lives to the
defense of freedom around the world.*

Text copyright © 1999 by Linda Granfield
Illustrations copyright © 1999 by Michael Martchenko

Published in Canada by Tundra Books, *McClelland & Stewart Young Readers*,
481 University Avenue, Toronto, Ontario M5G 2E9

Published in the United States by Tundra Books of Northern New York,
P.O. Box 1030, Plattsburgh, New York 12901

Library of Congress Catalog Number: 99-70971

Canadian Cataloguing in Publication Data

Granfield, Linda
    High flight : a story of World War II

ISBN 978-0-88776-469-1

1. Magee, John, 1922-1941 – Juvenile literature. 2. Magee, John, 1922-1941. High flight.
3. World War, 1939-1945 – Poetry. 4. World War, 1939-1945 – England – Juvenile literature. 5. Poets – 20th century – Biography – Juvenile literature. 6. Canada. Royal Canadian
Air Force – Biography – Juvenile literature. 7. Air pilots, Military – Biography – Juvenile
literature. I. Martchenko, Michael. II. Title.

PR6025.A3895Z7 13 12 11   j821'.912   C99-930555-7

We acknowledge the support of the Canada Council for the Arts and the Ontario Arts
Council for our publishing program.

We acknowledge the financial support of the Government of Canada through the Book
Publishing Industry Development Program for our publishing activities.

Canadä

Design by Sari Ginsberg

Printed and bound in Hong Kong, China

ACKNOWLEDGMENTS

The author and illustrator express heartfelt thanks to David B. Magee of New York. This book could not have been produced without his generosity of time, spirit, and materials regarding his brother John.

We also express our gratitude to the following people, who graciously contributed information and expertise: Rusty MacLean, Librarian, and Graham J. Hedges, Director of Communications, Rugby School, England; Marvin Kranz, Library of Congress, Washington, D.C.; Alf Pyner and the many World War II veterans who volunteer at the Canadian Warplane Heritage Museum, Hamilton, Ontario and the Royal Canadian Air Force Memorial Museum, Trenton, Ontario; Anne Immekus, Magee-Womens Hospital, Pittsburgh, Pennsylvania; Christopher Magee Steel; June Callwood; Chris Spence; Franny Magee; Richard Bentham; Henry Coons, Director of Alumni Affairs, Avon Old Farms School, Connecticut; Yale University; Anne Donaldson, Ireland; Imax Corporation; Lorelie Mitchell and Gail Einarson-McCleery, Icelandic-Canadian Club of Toronto; Vera Garthoff; Michael Aidin; Edyth McKitrick, Grace Church in New York; Timothy Dubé, National Archives of Canada; Virginia and Lucy Kirks; Cici Hughes; Greg Mounts of McClain, Dewey & Mounts Real Estate, Washington, D.C.; St. Augustine's Seminary, Toronto; Christine Reynolds, Westminster Abbey Library, London; Marc G. Ducharme, Registrar, the National Aviation Museum, Ottawa, Canada; Alyson Hudson, *Pittsburgh Post-Gazette;* Rev. Hugh E. Brown III, Mary Kelly, and Tim Heitmann of St John's Church, Washington, D.C.; Tangmere Aviation Museum, Chichester, England; Marv Cross, the United States Air Force Museum, Ohio; Barry Chad, Carnegie Library of Pittsburgh; Dr. Jean Marmoreo; the National Aeronautics and Space Administration (NASA); Chuck Zimkas, U.S. Space Foundation, Colorado; Captain Earl Hewison, CAF Ret'd, former Curator of the RCAF Memorial Museum, Trenton, Ontario; Captain Bruce Taylor, Blair Peterson, and Trena Lefevre, SkyWest Airlines; Bernie Goedhart; Warren Carroll; Richard Briggs; Barbara L. Cole, Imperial War Museum, Fighter Collection, Duxford, England; Mike Filey; Kathy Lowinger and the Tundra 'crew': Sue Tate, Lynn Paul, and Catherine Mitchell; Cal and Devon Smiley, who "chased the shouting wind along" on the home front, and Brian Smiley, who, for a few hot summer hours, posed as Pilot Officer John Magee.

Thanks as well go to F/L Fred Heather, Harry Lyon, Patrick Stoker, and the late "Terk" Bayly (Canada), Douglas Eves (England), and Rev. Trevor Hoy (United States), who knew John. Special thanks to John's brothers Christopher W. Magee and Reverend F. Hugh Magee (United States), who shared their personal recollections of him and took the time to read the manuscript.

And, finally, thank you to the many historians, photographers, and artists who have passionately chronicled the lives of those who survived, and honored the memories of those who perished during World War II.

HIGH FLIGHT

Oh! I have slipped the surly bonds of Earth
And danced the skies on laughter-silvered wings;
Sunward I've climbed, and joined the tumbling mirth
Of sun-split clouds, – and done a hundred things
You have not dreamed of – wheeled and soared and swung
High in the sunlit silence. Hov'ring there,
I've chased the shouting wind along, and flung
My eager craft through footless halls of air. . . .

Up, up the long, delirious, burning blue
I've topped the wind-swept heights with easy grace
Where never lark, or even eagle flew –
And, while with silent, lifting mind I've trod
The high untrespassed sanctity of space,
Put out my hand, and touched the face of God.

John G. Magee

3.ix.41

How old do you have to be to leave your mark? And what field would you enter to affect people's lives? Politics, perhaps, or teaching, or medicine?

This is the story of a youth, barely out of high school, who is remembered for a handful of words. His legacy is a poem, only fourteen lines long, that has been read, admired, and memorized by millions around the world – and beyond. Only months before he died, a fighter pilot aged nineteen, John Magee sent his poem "High Flight" to his parents. He hoped for, but never knew, the lasting impact his few words would have. Tragically, he lost his future in a terrible war.

For anyone who has ever flown, or who has looked with wonder at the sky, this is the story of the pilot poet.

John Gillespie Magee, Jr. was born in Shanghai, China on June 9, 1922, the son of missionaries John and Faith Magee. He and his two younger brothers, David and Christopher, had a comfortable life. Their nanny took them to school, and their cook sculpted tigers and elephants from the deep snow that fell. They played with the local children, and John learned to speak Chinese. When he turned nine, plans were made to send him far away to an English boarding school. In 1931, John, with his mother and two brothers, set out on the six-week voyage to England. Reverend Magee stayed behind in China to continue his mission work, and, during the next few years, the boys depended on his letters for reminders of their father's love.

John felt at home in the quiet green English countryside. Grandmother Backhouse lived in a house called Foxburrow, near Deal, in Kent. The surrounding area was filled with castles and historical sites that fascinated a boy newly arrived from China. At St. Clare School, young John studied Latin and Greek, as well as history. In school and at home, John was a lively, intelligent boy prone to pranks. While he was at St. Clare's, his youngest brother, Frederick Hugh, was born in 1933.

John's love of language blossomed when he entered the world-famous Rugby School at the age of fourteen. There, he wrote short pieces of fiction and humor, poetry, and reviews of school plays for Rugby's literary magazine. He admired the poetry of Rupert Brooke, a Rugby graduate who died young in the First World War.

Some of John's early writing was ordinary, or pretentious. Other pieces, however, glimmered with a surprisingly mature sense of style and observation. In a poem called "Lines Written on a Sleepless Night," he wrote: "I love to think I hear an angel's voice / Hung on the whisper of the wind." His teachers encouraged John. Like Rupert Brooke before him, John won the Rugby School Poetry Prize.

John was growing into a handsome youth, brimming with life. His study-mate called him a "genius daredevil," who reveled equally in jokes and books. On weekends, they walked the countryside, sailed down canals, and spent their small weekly allowance on sweets at a shop called The Stodge.

John was a proud member of Rugby's Officers Training Corps. Like other teenage boys, he was intrigued by the idea of love and all the joy and heartache that a first "crush" can bring. Though he wrote in a poem about disliking "the adhesive kiss of lipstick," he would have been happy for such a kiss from Elinor Lyon, the headmaster's daughter.

Beyond the peaceful grounds of Rugby, the world was in chaos. During the 1930s, the Great Depression left families and nations destitute. Reverend Magee displayed heroism in the defense of Nanking against the Japanese invasion of China. Civil war raged in Spain; the Great Terror engulfed Russia; the German dictator, Adolf Hitler, waited to pounce on Europe.

Despite the gathering war clouds in 1939, John enjoyed a carefree summer. He sailed to America and visited his father's sister, Aunt Mary Scaife, in Pittsburgh. The season was packed with parties, girls, horseback riding, and a visit to the New York World's Fair.

In the autumn, John began a year of studies at Avon Old Farms, a private boys' school in Connecticut. At Avon, John was a member of the crew and soccer squads. He used the school's printing facilities, and self-published a small book of poems. Although an American citizen by birth, John's British accent distinguished him from his classmates. His attitude did, too. The student who wrote about John in the yearbook was sarcastic: "He has exerted his poetic personality to the nth degree . . ." and "[John's] principal activities are sleeping, thinking, and commenting on the oddities of the Avon existence."

By the end of summer 1939, Hitler's troops had invaded Czechoslovakia and Poland. England and France declared war on Germany on the third of September. Country after country and, finally, France fell to the German army. World War II had begun.

John graduated with honors from Avon in the spring of 1940. He was accepted by Yale University and offered a scholarship to study classics. He spent the summer enjoying the beaches of Martha's Vineyard, off the coast of Massachusetts, and tutoring local students in Latin.

The newspapers reported German air attacks on England. Bombs were dropped near Foxburrow. The Battle of Britain, the world's first battle to be fought entirely in the air, was raging. John was eager to defend the place he called home. He asked to postpone his studies, and tried unsuccessfully to return to England. The United States had not entered the war and, like many other young men, John was afraid that if he didn't hurry, the war would be over without him. By joining the Royal Canadian Air Force (RCAF), he knew he could fight for England.

The Magees reluctantly granted their consent to eighteen-year-old John to join the RCAF. When he could have been entering Yale as a carefree undergraduate, John Magee was filling out enlistment forms and undergoing a medical examination. Over six feet tall, John was told he was sixteen pounds underweight. Two weeks later, the recruitment office deemed his weight acceptable.

In Montreal, Canada, on October 10, 1940, John Gillespie Magee, Jr. swore to serve as an American in the RCAF "for the duration of the present war. . . ." The Battle of Britain had been won by the British in September; anxious John Magee wouldn't be flying over the English countryside for nearly another year.

Manning Depot No. 1 in Toronto was Aircraftman 2nd Class John Magee's first taste of air force life. He learned military rules and a new vocabulary of "scrambles" and "ops." He lived without privacy. He slept on a bunk bed, surrounded by hundreds of snoring men. The boardwalk and dance halls along Lake Ontario provided diversions for John and his new friends. There they strolled and met young women eager to dance with men in uniform.

Trenton and St. Catharine's, Ontario were among John's stations during his training. They were part of the British Commonwealth Air Training Plan (BCATP), an arrangement between Canada and Britain for the training of aircrews. The "Plan" produced thousands of personnel for the war.

Young men like John Magee were exactly what the air force wanted for fighter pilots. They were in good health and eager for adventure. They were risk takers who could be trained to direct their energy against the enemy in the air. Some were surprised to learn that hours of classroom work in armament, mathematics, and meteorology were part of the course. The men studied hard because "you knew if you failed, it would cost you your life." Every student feared the ultimate shame of being "washed out," or asked to leave.

Trainees learned to fly in a Link trainer, which veterans say did all the bad things a plane could do except crash. There were flights in real planes with instructors and, finally, solo trips. Airmen practiced climbing 25,000 feet in the air, formation flying, spinning, firing, forced landings, and night flying. When not guarding old planes, or monotonously marching, the men scrubbed their socks and underwear and spit-polished their boots.

The officers' reports described John as a mixture of maturity and reckless-ness. The positive comments included: "very good pilot prospect" and "good on instrument and aerobatics." Less than commendable: he "lacks discipline," is "somewhat overconfident," and "not over popular with fellow classmates." John's friends remember him differently. They liked the young man with the high-pitched voice who thought he could do anything, who laughed, and made *them* laugh.

Like many of the airmen, John grew a pencil-thin mustache. He enjoyed parties on base and he flirted with the girls at the local steam laundry. None of his friends knew he wrote poetry, or had won an important poetry prize. To them, he was "a wild kid" in love with life and all it had to offer.

Many servicemen kept in touch with their families through letters, but everyone looked forward to "leave," short visits away. At Christmas 1940, John traveled to Washington, D.C. to visit his family. His father had completed his mission work and was the assistant minister at St. John's Church, known as "The Church of the Presidents."

The Magees rented a lovely townhouse on tree-lined Bancroft Place. It was a home filled with long banisters for Hugh to slide down, and window seats to dream in. For John, the house and the city were brand-new places to explore. Washington was full of history and heroes.

The sight of a RCAF airman walking down Washington's streets was rare and John enjoyed the attention. His parents listened as he described his life in Canada. They saw that their rebellious son was benefiting from the discipline. Brother David heard about the social life John was enjoying. While for several years John had expressed doubts about religion, on Christmas Day he attended church with his pleased family.

Soon John was back in Canada, flying in bright yellow training planes. He made serious flying mistakes, broke rules, and suffered the consequences. By March 1941, he was in Ottawa, at Uplands base, completing the last of his training. Once, he made a no-gas landing miles from the city and had to walk back to Ottawa. He was still listed by his commanding officers as an above-average flying student with good instincts. However, lapses in conduct and overconfidence were reminders that John Magee was a talented teen, not a mature man.

John was a happy fellow on June 16, 1941, when he received his "wings," his pilot's flying badge, during a wings parade. He later reported to his family that he believed he was flying one of the planes passing overhead as a Hollywood director filmed the parade for the Jimmy Cagney movie *Captains of the Clouds*.

John spent a final few days' leave in Washington. He cheered when a telegram arrived notifying him of his commission as a pilot officer. In July he would embark for England. On the summer's day when John left Washington, the Magee family hugged and kissed their son and brother, not knowing that it was their last time together.

On July 5, 1941, John left Halifax on the HMS *California,* bound for Iceland and the RCAF transit station at Keflavik. During the week of waiting there, John and some friends packed their lunch and hiked over the lichen-covered rocks of Thingvellir. Soon it was time to board a boat for a dangerous trip to England. German U-boats could attack at any time; however, the friends landed safely.

John and a friend rode to Bournemouth in a train so crowded they climbed into the luggage racks to sleep. The racks broke. By mid-August, John was in Wales training in Spitfires, the fighter planes of the Battle of Britain.

Airstrips were runways cut through fields. Some were paved, others just soil and stones. Hangars reeked of oil and paint thinner. Planes smelled of gas and vomit as unsteady pilots practiced dives. Movies made pilots look like solo heroes, but real pilots couldn't do their jobs without the ground crews who spent all night repairing planes, and who were up in the morning before the pilots. The crews warmed up the oil in the engines and tested the equipment one last time. They strapped a pilot into the cockpit and waved good-bye.

It was cold flying thousands of feet in the sky in a plane with no insulation. Pilots wore layers of clothing, including a brown fleece coverall called a teddy-bear suit. They wore scratchy blue-gray wool pants and jackets, topped by a "Mae West," a vest named for a famous buxom actress. A helmet and gloves, scarf and boots, microphone and headphones, oxygen mask and very uncomfortable parachute that a pilot sat on completed the outfit.

A tall pilot like John had to squeeze into the cockpit so that the bubble canopy could be closed over his head. The pilot's shoulders were crammed between the walls of the plane, and the trembling control column, or "stick," rose from the floor between his legs. As one veteran airman said, the efficient cockpit was so small "you belonged to it."

By mid-September 1941, John was posted to No. 412 (RCAF) Fighter Squadron at Wellingore, near Digby, in Lincolnshire. In November, he experienced his first air battle, near Dunkirk, France. As John dodged and fired at enemy planes, he watched as his squadron leader and friends were shot from the sky.

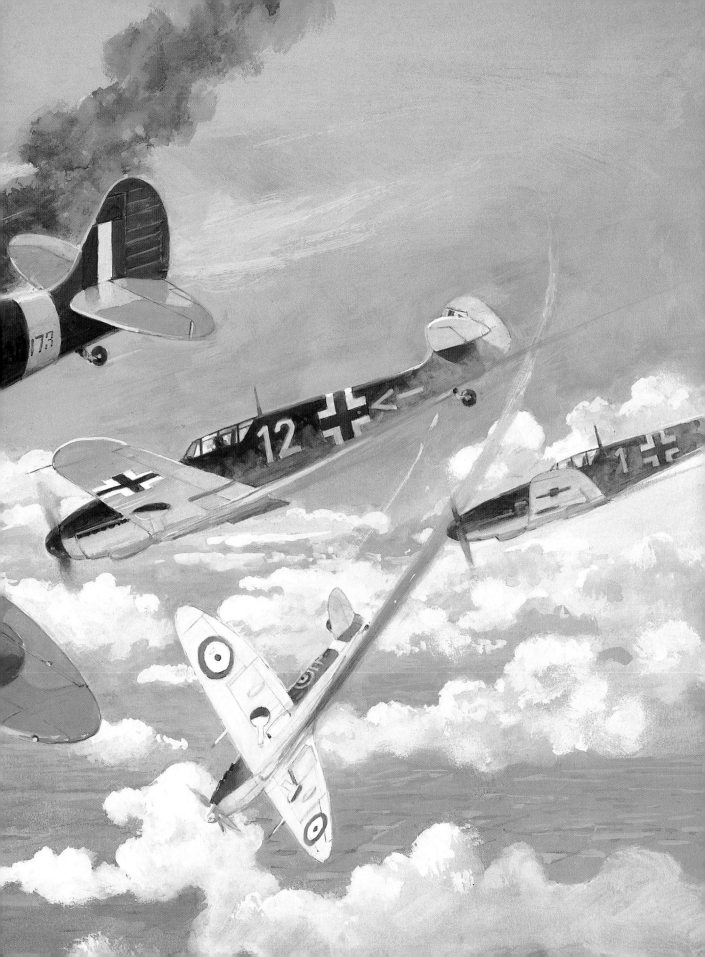

British citizens were greatly affected by the war. Windows were covered with "blackout" curtains at night, so enemy planes would not see them. Vegetables replaced inedible garden flowers. Houses without cellars soon had corrugated steel shelters in the garden.

Often during the war, children from large English cities that were enemy targets were sent into the countryside for safety. Everyone was warned not to leave home without gas masks – children kept them handy at play and at school.

Clothing changed as certain fabrics became unavailable and items were reserved for military use. For example, only nine buttons were allowed on a woman's dress. (After the war, the plastic windscreens of old warplanes were recycled into buttons for dresses.) Inferior leather was used for shoes, clothes were patched, and nylon stockings were rare as nylon was used to make parachutes for the airmen. The thread from the top of manure bags (needed in the "Dig for Victory" gardens) was used to darn heavy stockings.

Limited food supplies meant that people did without, or became very creative. Cakes were made with little sugar and no eggs. When John Magee arrived in England, a person was allotted one egg (in its shell) each month. People used dried eggs and powdered milk, which came in tin cans. Fats, like margarine, became so scarce they were applied as thinly as possible – with a shaving brush.

Ration books filled with tiny coupons were important items in the wartime home. Without them, a family couldn't get food, clothing, or petrol (gas) for the car. Mothers went to the fields and factories to take over jobs the men left behind. There was scrap metal and lard and used newspapers and rags to be collected for recycling as bomb linings and pieces of airplanes. Children donated their metal toys to be melted down with the beautiful railings and gates from the parks.

Families watched the vapor trails made overhead as British and German planes fought above England. Pieces of planes, and even enemy pilots, fell from the sky. Children mimicked the war around them by inventing secret codes and looking for "the enemy" among the ruins on their streets. Sadly, for many children, the long war robbed them of family members and changed their lives forever.

For hundreds of years before the air battles of World Wars I and II, people wanted to fly like the birds. In 1927, just before John Magee's fifth birthday, Charles A. Lindbergh made the first solo nonstop transatlantic flight. It took nearly thirty-four hours; today, the same flight can take less than four hours.

By the time World War II began in 1939, some people had been passengers on commercial flights. Young men like John had sat in movie theaters and watched dashing pilots, like Errol Flynn and David Niven in films like *Dawn Patrol* (1938), fly into the skies and return as heroes. The war made their dreams a nightmarish reality.

In his Spitfire, Pilot Officer John Magee flew solo flights over the green hills of England. Gathering speed and altitude, he moved through layers of sunlit, billowing clouds that formed gray ceilings frosted with white. Despite the racket made by the plane's machinery, the sky offered peace. This was time for a pilot to be alone with his thoughts, to feel free from the turmoil below.

In September 1941, one of John's many letters home described the result of such a flight: "I am enclosing a verse I wrote the other day. It started at 30,000 feet, and was finished soon after I landed. I thought it might interest you." He continued to say: "I think we are very lucky as we shall just be in time for the autumn blitzes [bombings] (which are certain to come)." John listed popular films that would give his family a glimpse of squadron life, and closed with: "I have no more news so will stop now. P.T.O. [please turn over] for Ditty."

Some ditty. On the reverse side of the blue paper, John neatly wrote the poem "High Flight" and dated it "September 3, 1941." John's parents shared the poem with friends at a church council meeting that month. It appears that proud Aunt Mary sent the poem to the *Pittsburgh Post-Gazette*. In the November 12th issue, "High Flight" was published in a column entitled "This World of Books." A footnote described John, his Pittsburgh connections, and the fact that "[he] is now serving in Great Britain."

In just a few weeks, "High Flight" would be known around the world.

John Magee joined the RCAF in 1940 because the United States was not yet involved in World War II. However, after 350 Japanese aircraft surprise-attacked the American naval base at Pearl Harbor, Hawaii, on December 7, 1941, the U.S. declared war on Japan. Hitler declared war on the United States; the American Congress, in turn, joined the war in Europe. The conflict was truly worldwide.

Four wintry days after Pearl Harbor, on December 11th, John Magee took off in his Spitfire to practice wing formation flying with a group of fellow pilots. While John was flying above the clouds, young Ernest Aubrey Griffin was in the air below, training in an Airspeed Oxford.

It was 11:30 a.m. As the Spitfires were letting down through the clouds to return to base, John Magee's plane collided with the Oxford only 1400 feet above the ground. Both planes went out of control. The silence of the sky was torn by the screeching of a crippled engine, the ripping of metal, and the whistling of air as John's plane hurtled to the earth.

At an inquiry, a farmer testified that he saw the Spitfire pilot struggle to push back the canopy. The pilot, he said, finally stood to jump from the plane. John, however, was too close to the ground for his parachute to open. He died instantly. His neck had broken when his body fell into the soft soil of the fields near a house called Roxholm Hall. Griffin died as his fiery plane crashed.

The next day, a telegram was delivered to Bancroft Place: "Deeply regret to inform you advice received from Royal Canadian Air Force Casualties Officer overseas. . . ." John was listed as "killed on active service." Thirteen-year-old Christopher Magee, a delivery boy for *The Washington Post*, knew he could telephone a reporter with news. "I thought – you might be interested," he said. "My older brother joined the Royal Canadian Air Force." The reporter waited. "Well – the telegram just came. . . . He's been killed in action." Izetta Winter Robb reported that John's parents "felt they had to be brave" and that Christopher said: "And we [John's brothers] intend to get in the air force the minute we're old enough!" Once again "High Flight" was printed in Pittsburgh, this time accompanied by a lament for the fallen.

The Magee family received a letter from the commanding officer of No. 412 Squadron. It described the funeral that had taken place so far away, and contained a photograph of the grave. John was buried on December 13th in Scopwick Cemetery, near the Digby Aerodrome. His brother officers and fellow airmen had provided the wreaths.

John's parents wrote to the Royal Canadian Air Force: ". . . we gave our consent and blessing to [John] as he left us to enter the RCAF. We felt as deeply as he did and we were proud of his determination and spirit. We knew that such news as did come might come. When his sonnet reached us we felt then that it had a message for American youth but did not know how to get it before them. Now his death has emblazoned it across the entire country. We are thinking that this may have been a greater contribution than anything he may have done in the way of fighting. . . .[we] will be forever proud of him."

Mrs. Magee comforted John's former studymate in another letter: ". . . I wish you had seen [John] after he had been for some months in the RCAF; the change in him was tremendous. He lost that dissatisfied and restless feeling which he had . . . and he found himself doing something which he really longed to do, and which he felt that he could do and do well. Everyone who saw him during the last few months in England speaks of his happiness. . . ."

Ten days after his death, John's "High Flight" was published in the St. John's Church bulletin. Parishioners were reminded that just one year before, John had taken communion there with his family. Now he had given "the last full measure of devotion." The original copy of the poem was soon on display at the Library of Congress in Washington (where it remains today) in an exhibit called "Poems of Faith and Freedom." It was already ranked by critics with John McCrae's "In Flanders Fields" and Rupert Brooke's "The Soldier," both World War I poems, as a superb example of war poetry.

Copies of a poster depicting the poem, a portrait of John, and a drawing of a Spitfire were sent to every airfield in the British Empire. Newspapers printed the sonnet. Airmen

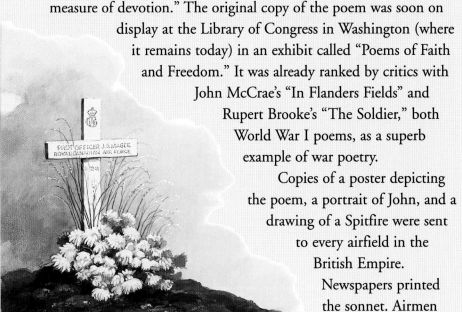

recognized that John had captured perfectly the intoxication of flight; clergy realized that the poem "had a message for the youth of America at this time."

The war was to drag on for nearly four more years, and servicemen and civilians alike needed words of inspiration to sustain them. When he was eighteen, David Magee joined the U.S. Army Air Corps and served as a bombardier on B-24 "Liberators."

The Magees comforted parish families who suffered the loss of their young men and women. ". . . we should tell the mothers of other boys not to grieve for them," Faith Magee wrote to a friend. "A few weeks ago . . . I felt [John] very near at the end of the service, and if I could have remained quietly, I think he would have talked to me. . . . That afternoon I was in the Cathedral again. . . . As we knelt again in the little chapel, John was there speaking of the fact that he and the other mother's son . . . were together. . . ."

Theater newsreels and the world's newspapers bombarded the public with images of war. Major battles were fought on the deserts of North Africa, in the jungles of Pacific islands, in snow-covered Russia and rain-soaked Italy. Place names like El Alamein and Midway were suddenly household words. So, too, were foreign words, like *kamikaze*, *blitzkrieg* and *Luftwaffe*.

In the early hours of June 6, 1944, thousands of Allied troops landed on the shores of Normandy and "D-Day," the largest land and sea invasion in history, began. By the end of the battle, more than 10,000 troops had perished, but the Allies had won. During the summer months, the enemy was in retreat and the end of the war in Europe was in sight.

In April, 1945, Berlin was captured and Adolf Hitler was dead. Germany surrendered on May 7th, and the next day was proclaimed "V-E (Victory in Europe) Day." Blackout curtains were pulled back, and lights beamed as people sang and danced in the streets.

Celebrations for the total end of war would have to wait until August, after U.S. planes dropped atomic bombs on Hiroshima and Nagasaki, Japan. The incredible devastation convinced the Japanese to surrender on the second of September. The war the young John Magee had hurried to join was finally over. The world had lost an estimated 64 million people in the conflict. David and Christopher Magee would be coming home, while John would not. The rebuilding of shattered countries and families began.

In the new year, the Magees moved from Washington to Connecticut, where Reverend Magee served as a chaplain at Yale University. David began his studies at Yale, where John had also planned to study after the war. Faith Magee recited "High Flight" at Sunday afternoon teas she held for students. A recording of her recitation can be heard at the U.S. Air Force Museum, in Dayton, Ohio. "Oh! I have slipped the surly bonds of Earth . . . ," she begins. Many listeners at the museum recite the rest of her son's legacy with her.

In 1944, Christopher Magee, a sixteen-year-old in the Combat Merchant Marine, stood on an oil tanker deck and heard actor Orson Welles's voice booming from the loud speaker: "I now want to recite for you what I believe to be the finest poem to have come out of this war, 'High Flight'. . . ." Christopher wept to hear his brother's words.

"High Flight" is, indeed, a greater contribution than anything John Magee accomplished in battle. The poem is an anthem for all aviators: war veterans, commercial aircraft pilots, even glider pilots. "High Flight" appeals to those who have soared in the clouds, and those who find consolation in a spiritual interpretation of the words. For these reasons, "High Flight" is often recited at ceremonies, or printed in air cadet handbooks and newspaper obituaries.

In 1971, Apollo 15 Lunar Module Pilot James Irwin carried a copy of "High Flight" to the same moon that John had gazed at from the windows of Foxburrow, Rugby, and Bancroft Place. President Ronald Reagan renewed interest in the teenage poet when he read lines from "High Flight" following the loss of seven astronauts aboard the space shuttle *Challenger*, in January 1986. When Alan Shepard, America's first man in space, died in 1998, "High Flight" was included in the many tributes to him.

John's poem has inspired a variety of musical compositions. Audiences have heard "High Flight" recited while they watched television sign-offs and IMAX screens seven stories high. The poem is quoted, often incorrectly, on hundreds of worldwide web sites. John once wrote to his parents: "If anyone should want this [poem] please see that it is accurately copied, capitalized, and punctuated."

"High Flight" informs and uplifts. It reminds us that a few words, even those written in youth, can hold great power. John Gillespie Magee, Jr. *was not* a fighting hero of World War II. He *was* a talented young man who, like many other youths lost in the war, showed great promise. John, as he wrote in a poem, was "[for] a short time dearly loved; and, after – slept." Sixty years later, "High Flight" continues to inspire and console. Like John Magee, the poem is a reflection on all that is full of promise, faith, hope, and joy.